British Railway Diesel Memori...

No. 84: The Western

Norman Preedy

Copyright Book Law Publications 2015

ISBN 978-1-909625-45-7

INTRODUCTION

My relationship with the mighty Western Class diesel-hydraulics really started in the summer of 1969. It is true to say however that long before then I had seen each member of the class and photographed a number of them whilst out and about photographing the ever dwindling British Railways steam locomotive fleet. At the end of the normal steam operations on BR in August 1968 I, like many others, put my camera away.

During a trip to Bristol in the summer of 1969 I saw a number of Westerns with their cast name and number plates and my interest was reawakened. I then set about spending all my spare time, and cash, photographing and riding behind them all across the Western Region, spending many happy hours doing so. My favourite photographic location has to be the sea wall between Dawlish Warren and Teignmouth where I took hundreds of pictures but, like all the good things, it had to come to an end!

The Western class went out in a blaze of glory with every train that they hauled packed with the followers of the graceful C-Cs. Several 'final' tours were run by various organisations, some even by BR. Most took in the lines over which the class had worked, some were double-headed and all were sold out as soon as they were announced!

The 'final' tour was organised by BR who aptly named it the WESTERN TRIBUTE which was set to run on Saturday 26th February 1977 and which took in all the routes over which the class had seen many years of service. The trip commenced appropriately at Paddington station and took in Swindon, Newport, Swansea, Bristol, Plymouth, Newbury, and Reading arriving back in Paddington at around 23:40 – a journey of 628 miles. The locomotives used on that epic journey were 1013 WESTERN RANGER and 1023 WESTERN FUSILLER with 1010 WESTERN CAMPAINGER and 1048 WESTERN LADY acting as the back-up team but in the event they were not required. Happily all four of those locomotives are now preserved along with sisters 1062 WESTERN COURIER, 1041 WESTERN PRINCE and 1015 WESTERN CHAMPION. The latter can often be seen at the head of charter trains on the main line running over familiar routes from the days when it was in frontline service; the others work on Heritage lines throughout the country.

I hope that you, the reader, will gain as much pleasure from this album as I did when putting it together. It brought back many happy WESTERN memories.

Norman Preedy, Gloucester, June 2015

(*Cover*) See page 56.

(*Title page*) **D1053 WESTERN PATRIARCH has left Westbury and is approaching Fairwood Junction in charge of 1B73, the 14.30 Paddington to Paignton express on 30th March 1974.**

Printed and bound by The Amadeus Press, Cleckheaton, West Yorkshire
First published in the United Kingdom by Book Law Publications, 382 Carlton Hill, Nottingham, NG4 1JA

In freezing conditions and with a carpet of snow covering the tracks D1000 WESTERN ENTERPRISE, the doyen of the class, nears Hatton with a Birkenhead to Paddington express in January 1963. The scene is typical of that terrible winter of 1962-63 with railwaymen working to free frozen points; the lines leading off to the left are for Stratford on Avon. D1000 is still in the desert sand livery which it carried from entering traffic in December 1961 until October 1964 when it was repainted into a standard maroon livery. Note the locomotive is carrying its unique aluminium 'lion and wheel' emblems.

(*opposite*) **D1001 WESTERN PATHFINDER** calls at Bodmin Road station with the **08.30 Cardiff to Penzance** express on **Saturday 31st July 1976**. British Railways had by this period discontinued the use of the four-digit train description numbers so the headcode panels were redundant and out of use. However, many of the class carried their fleet numbers in the vacant spaces as 1001 is doing here; this made it easy to identify a locomotive on approach. The Westerns did a lot of fine work in Cornwall amidst the superb scenery and it was great to ride behind them over the route from Plymouth to Penzance. Bodmin Road is named Bodmin Parkway nowadays and is the terminus for the Bodmin & Wenford heritage railway which has a passenger platform and run round loop at the station.

D1002 WESTERN EXPLORER stands 'On the Blocks' at Paddington after arrival with 1A58 from the West Country on the 3rd March 1971. This photograph was taken as a time exposure using a tripod and a long exposure without the need for using flash which would attract unwanted attention. It must be said the staff at Paddington were very good about photography after dark and I got to know a lot of them during my many visits there. The 'shedplate' carried by D1002 was located to the right of the nearest cab door and comprised a small square transfer with the legend 84A beneath LAIRA. As an aside, note the copious amounts of planking beneath the roof – either the painters or the cleaners were installed!

D1003 WESTERN PIONEER at Fairwood Junction near Westbury on 1A45, the 06.30 Penzance to Paddington service. The tracks on the far right lead into Westbury station and the yards whilst our subject is on the avoiding line. Fairwood was a superb location but has now changed out of all the recognition from what is depicted here; the signal box is long gone whilst the elm trees behind it were felled after they became victims of disease.

D1004 WESTERN CRUSADER stabled on one of the old turntable stalls at Old Oak Common on the Saturday 24th February 1973. Up to this date the class was intact but during the following May the first withdrawals would take place when D1019 and D1032 were condemned. D1004 was called in during August and it didn't stop there; by the end of the year eleven of the class had gone. For the record six of them were Swindon-built. Interestingly, for those into statistics for instance, two each month went in May, June, July, August, and November; October saw just 1038 succumb! As if repeating history, eleven also went the following year whereas 1975 saw seventeen chopped: unlike the 'Warships' they were resisting total annihilation – for now! One of the named Brush 47s, 1660 CITY OF TRURO, stands on the next stall.

(*opposite*) **D1005 WESTERN VENTURER** is seen under the Paddington roof after arrival in platform 2 with 1A45 the 12.40 Penzance to Paddington express on 12th March 1976. The head code panel appears to be in a right mess with jumbled characters.

D1006 WESTERN STALWART stands at Gloucester on the 28th November 1965; beneath the filth, the locomotive is in maroon livery with half yellow warning panels. It is of interest that this particular C-C – along with sister D1039 – was the subject of an experiment which involved the fitting of a G. Kent Ltd. 'Clear View Screen' and associated washing equipment which was located to the screen on driving side of the cabs at both ends; I seem to remember the experiment was commissioned to start from about Friday 5th November 1965 – weather permitting! Although the equipment worked well, experiment was not deemed to be a success because of the complexity of the circular marine-type revolving screens. No further members of the class – or indeed any diesel class - were so fitted although an EM2 electric locomotive on the Manchester-Sheffield-Wath line was similarly equipped. However, it was to be sometime in 1967 before the experimental equipment was removed and normal widescreen wipers – and screens – re-instated. On the day before this picture was captured on film, D1006 was used to haul BR's last steam special between Gloucester and Cheltenham (St James) station, whilst 'Castle' No.7029 CLUN CASTLE was being serviced at Gloucester Horton Road shed in readiness to return the special back to Paddington.

D1007 WESTERN TALISMAN at Gloucester (Eastgate) with the lunchtime Cheltenham to Paddington service on 22nd May 1969. The locomotive is in the maroon livery with the half yellow warning panels. Eastgate station is no more, now being the site of an Asda Superstore! All rail traffic is now concentrated on what was the Central station, the drawback here is that many trains have to reverse to continue their journey expect, of course, those bound for South Wales. D1007 was involved in a serious accident whilst hauling the 17.18 express from Paddington to Oxford on the evening of 19th December 1973; the locomotive was derailed, along with some of the coaches, whilst travelling at speed between Ealing Broadway and West Ealing. The cause of the accident was traced to the door on the battery box which had been left unlocked and fell open shortly into the journey and hit a point operating machine. The points then moved beneath D1007, throwing it onto its side whilst derailing the coaches which then came to rest across the tracks. Sadly some ten people lost their lives and many more were injured.

(*opposite*) D1008 WESTERN HARRIER at Reading (General) on 8th June 1973 working 1A55, the 09.55 Paignton to Paddington service. This view, taken from the Southern Region platform – notice the 3rd rail – shows the old Reading station which has undergone a total rebuild during the last couple of years.

D1009 WESTERN INVADER approaches Fairwood Junction from Westbury, on 6th July 1974 whilst working one of the many stone trains that plied to and from the quarries in this area. The wagons were the property of Foster Yeomen and most likely headed to Merehead quarry. Westbury was a good spot for seeing the Westerns at work because, apart from the mainline trains, they were used quite a lot on these mineral workings. The avoiding line is to the right.

D1010 WESTERN CAMPAIGNER leaving Parsons Tunnel between Dawlish and Teignmouth on 1B39, the 10.56 Paddington to Penzance express on 2nd August 1975. This stretch of railway is most photogenic and attracted many photographers as it is also very close to the sea; on occasions there have been washouts in the high tides of Spring and Autumn. During the winter of 2014 a serious washout caused the line to be closed for a couple of months and effectively cut-off the rail network serving most of Devon and all of Cornwall. D1010 is now preserved, in working order, on the West Somerset Railway at Minehead. Meanwhile nothing has been done regarding the possible future weather related isolation of the same areas that were affected in 2014. We live in the age of a wing and a prayer!

(*opposite*) **D1011 WESTERN THUNDERER arrives at Gloucester Yard on the 18th June 1975 working 6V53, the 04.27 Stoke-on-Trent to St Blazey empty china clay wagons; the Western would have taken the train – with about sixty wagons in tow – over in Bescot yard from another diesel which had worked in from Stoke. Always a popular train with the photographers this one as there were not a lot of freight trains in the south-west of England during that period of BR history.**

D1012 WESTERN FIREBAND gets away from the Exeter (St David's) stop with 1B25, the 08.30 Paddington to Penzance service on the 1st June 1971. Of interest is yet another experiment tried out on five of the class with a view to improving cab ventilation by supplying a direct flow of air from the square grill on the front panel of the locomotive. The other Westerns involved were: D1028, D1039, D1056 and D1071. The air flow equipment was fitted at some period around 1967 and remained with the C-Cs throughout their lives. No other members of the class were so equipped so, was it a success or not?

(*opposite*) **D1013 WESTERN RANGER** at Paddington station on Friday 9th July 1976 whilst working the 16.53 Paddington to Penzance express. This service was one of the trains which had a Westbury stop and did not use the avoiding line. If one was on a Western Region Rover ticket, this train (if 'Western' hauled of course) gave a good run to Plymouth in time for supper and a ride back to Paddington on the overnight; a trip which I made several times! D1013 was a popular participant on rail tours and was involved in the final BR **WESTERN TRIBUTE** tour of 26th February 1977. Note the shed code LA (Laira) composed of a transfer applied to the cab-side above the numberplate; quite a transition from the cast iron shed plates of the steam era. D1013 is now preserved in working order and can be seen from time to time on the Severn Valley Railway.

D1014 WESTERN LEVIATHAN enters St David's station Exeter on 18th July 1971 with 4B09, the 16.00 Bristol to Plymouth van train. There would be a stop at Exeter for station staff to load and offload parcels. So, where did that traffic disappear too?

D1015 WESTERN CHAMPION leaves Bristol (Parkway) with 1A43 the 08.53 Swansea to Paddington service on 7th April 1973. Out-shopped from Swindon during January 1963, D1015 was treated to a one-off Golden Ochre livery which it carried until November 1965, when it was repainted into the then standard maroon livery. Its external condition in this image looks to be the work of painters rather than cleaners of a washing plant. This Western is also preserved in full working order and is used often on rail tours on the main line, and visiting places it would never have done during its BR career. The area has now been built up quite extensively since this picture was taken and there is also a Freightliner office and stabling point on the land to the left of the picture.

On 20th June 1974, D1016 WESTERN GLADIATER powers through Dawlish and out onto the seawall towards Dawlish Warren in charge of 1A69 the 08.40 Penzance to Paddington express. This is near to the spot were the two major washouts spectacularly occurred during the high tides of winter 2014.

(opposite) **D1017 WESTERN WARRIOR** rounds the curve at Dawlish Warren in charge of 1B45, the 10.30 Paddington to Penzance service on 18th July 1971. The Secondman is seen getting a breath of sea air on what was a very hot day. D1017 was one of only four members of the class not to be dual-braked with the fitting of air-brakes; it remained a vacuum only machine. This particular locomotive, along with similarly fitted D1018, D1019 and D1020 were withdrawn from service as early as May, June and August 1973 – basically the first lot to go. The WR obviously decided that seventy dual braked members would do for the remaining life of the class.

D1018 WESTERN BUCCANEER, another of the vacuum braked members of the class, departs from the south end of Exeter (St Davids) station on train 1C60 from Paddington to the West of England on Thursday 9th July 1970. D1018 is in quite a poor state externally and seems to have suffered a 'side swipe' at some time recently as besides a dent running along the lower body, a number of the nameplate letters and most of its border are missing after a similar coming-together!

D1019 WESTERN CHALLENGER stands at Horton Road depot in Gloucester on 19th April 1970; another member of the class stands close by whilst a Hymek Type 3 is seen in the background. D1019 was withdrawn during May 1973 becoming the first of the vacuum braked Westerns to go, the first Western, and the first of the Swindon-built machines to succumb! Without ceremony, she was cut up at Swindon Works during October 1974. Those Westerns which were modified for hauling air-braked stock (principally the Mark 2 coaching stock which the WR received from 1968) were fitted from 1968 onwards and to enable the Westinghouse compressor to be located within the already cramped confines of the locomotive body, a fuel tank with a capacity of 272 gallons had to be removed. The associated air tanks were positioned in gangways, bolted onto the two Maybach engines, and fixed so as to hang from the engine room roof supports! A bit of a mish-mash to say the least but necessary in the circumstances! The original vacuum-ejector brake handles on the driving consoles were replaced by new handles to operate the air brakes, and when necessary, the vacuum brake. A switch-over handle to change from air-to-vacuum mode was located in the engine room. Passage through the engine room of the converted locomotives from one cab to the other was now virtually impossible because of the new air associated equipment; luckily the switch-over handle was within easy reach. Note no shed code transfers on either of these two.

(*opposite, top*) D1020 WESTERN HERO at Bristol on a dull Thursday 17th July 1969. The Laira based Western had arrived at Temple Meads on 1E21, the 10.25 Penzance to Bradford Inter-Regional cross-country working. The train was then taken forward by a 'Peak' or Class 47; I failed to note which. Making its way onto Bath Road shed, D1020 would now be ready to head back south on another Inter-Regional train. Once again a Hymek can be seen to the left whilst another Western is already on the depot, possibly as the standby locomotive. Evidence of the cast shedplate – probably 82A Bristol from where it had just transferred – formerly carried by D1020 can be seen on the side skirt nearest the camera.

(*opposite bottom*) Another aspect of D1020 WESTERN HERO, stabled at Horton Road depot on 17th July 1969.

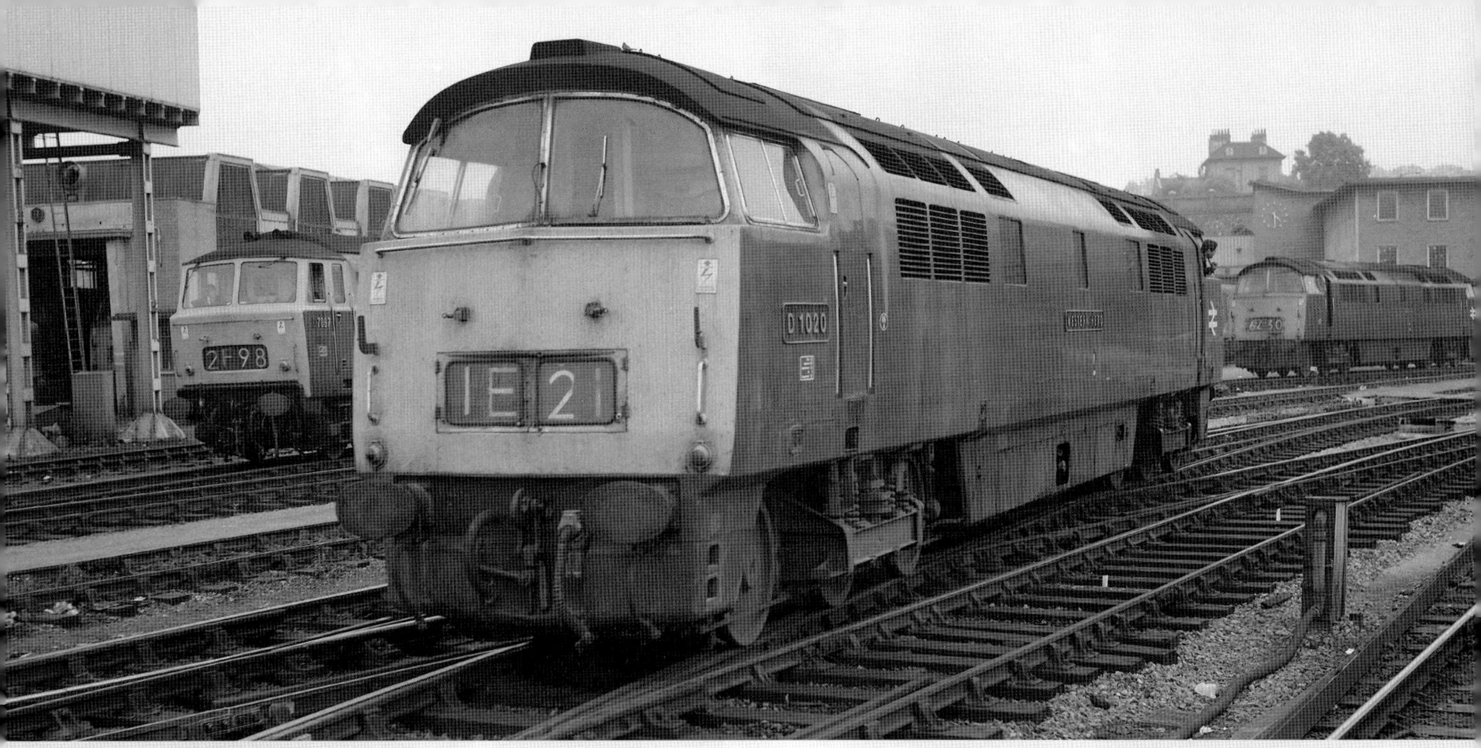
2F98
D1020
1E 21

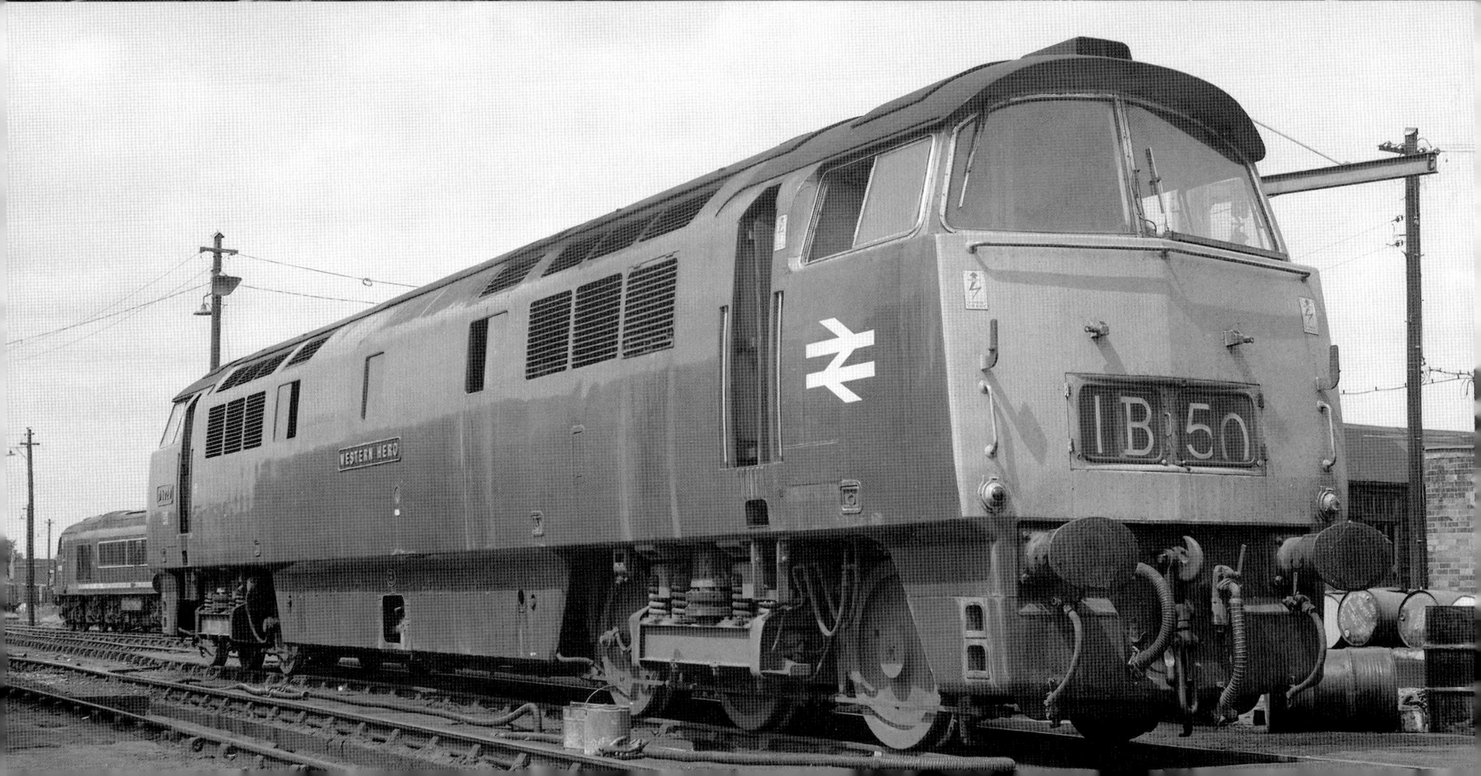
WESTERN HERO
1B 50

D1021 WESTERN CAVALIER pauses at Newton Abbot with 1B05 (which was the incorrect head code) the 08.35 Paddington to Plymouth express on Sunday 24th August 1975. In my notes I see that I was hauled from Bristol behind D1021 so the train was routed from Paddington via Bristol. A group of Western fans also left the train here.

D1022 WESTERN SENTINEL on shed at Exeter Riverside in the company of a Peak Class 45 awaiting their next turns of duty on 6th July 1975. This stabling point (SP) was on the site of the former Great Western and later Western Region steam shed which was coded 83C in the old Newton Abbot division. Dating from 1864 and opened by the Bristol & Exeter Railway, the steam shed – long since roofless - was closed to steam in October 1963 and was immediately improvised for stabling diesel locomotives. Long after the Westerns had gone, a single road shed was built on this site for servicing diesel locomotives. Note the oil pollution soaked around the tracks.

D1023 WESTERN FUSILIER at Reading on 27th December 1975 at the head of 1B43, the 18.30 Paddington to Penzance service. Once again the locomotive is unable to show the correct head code because the blinds have become jammed. D1023 was involved in the mammoth Western Tribute Tour of 26th February 1977. Claimed for the National Collection, WESTERN FUSILIER is in full working order and when not out on the road or visiting Heritage sites, can be seen at the National Railway Museum at York. This locomotive was the last of the class to be dual-braked, an event which was preceded by the first withdrawals!

D1024 WESTERN HUNTSMAN takes a breather in between duties at Horton Road depot Gloucester, 20th May 1970. Its next job will be the afternoon Cheltenham to Paddington service, the stock for which it will take over from Gloucester. D1024 entered traffic on 18th October 1963, working initially from Canton depot but was transferred to Bristol on 22nd June 1964. Quite an early casualty with just ten years service under its belt, the C-C was withdrawn on 17th November 1973, and cut up at Swindon during the following August. The home shed of this machine at the time when this image was recorded was Laira and the oval shaped (steam age) shed code plate with 84A inside the border can be seen painted on the body side to the right of the cab door.

D1025 WESTERN GUARDSMAN at Paddington station on 7th December 1974 with an evening departure for Swansea - 1C83? Again a tripod and a long time exposure were employed to get this image on film. Initially working from Canton depot – the seventh 'Western' to be allocated to Cardiff from new – D1025 was one of the last five remaining Swindon-built machines at this time and entered traffic on 2nd November 1963 without any headboard clips as can be seen in this view – D1026 to D1029 were similarly turned-out. The 'D' prefix has been painted over but it was still there, as large as life. Note the square LA shed code transfer on the cab side.

D1026 WESTERN CENTURION on the seawall stretch of line near Dawlish on a hot 20th June 1974. The diesel is working an E.C.S move judging by the 5Z70 head code. D1026 lasted into another summer but was withdrawn in October 1975 along with six other members of the class – the worse month on record for Western class withdrawals.

D1027 WESTERN LANCER arrives at Truro on 3rd July 1975. This train was a relief working from Penzance to Birmingham and the head code should perhaps read 1Z16. LANCER would take the train through to Bristol where it would be replaced by a Peak or Brush Class 47 as it was not often that a Western was seen in Birmingham unless it had arrived on a Paddington to Birmingham service. Even then it was sent back to London on a return working as soon as possible. This view, looking west and taken from the footbridge at the station, reveals a couple of modern warehouses which had been recently built on the site of Truro's engine shed – 83F – which closed in November 1965.

D1028 WESTERN HUSSAR is seen at Tramway Crossing Gloucester on 7V69 to Severn Tunnel Junction on 5th April 1969. D1028 is still in the maroon livery with a half yellow warning panel, the train would shortly pass through Gloucester (Central) station and continue on through Lydney and Chepstow. This route is also very scenic as it runs along the River Severn near Lydney for quite some distance - a mini seawall, if you like!

D1029 WESTERN LEGIONNAIRE arrives at Bristol (Temple Meads) at the head of 1M54, the 11.35 Penzance to Nottingham (Midland) on Saturday 2nd August 1969. D1029, one of Bath Road's own, would be removed here in favour of a Peak or Class 47 for the rest of the run to Nottingham. In the background can be seen a Warship Class 42 D866 ZEBRA acting as the standby motive power. This Western was not only the last of the Swindon built locomotives; she was also the last of the class to enter service – 4th May 1964 – although not because of any shortcomings within the Swindon factory. It had been retained so that a number of comparison tests and trials associated with the class, diesel-hydraulics, and diesel-electrics could be undertaken by Swindon's testing unit. I wonder how they went?

(*opposite*) **D1030 WESTERN MUSKETEER** at Reading with 1A43, the 08.53 Swansea to Paddington express on 2nd March 1974. D1030 was amongst the last of the Crewe-built machines and entered traffic on the last day of 1963 along with D1031 and D1032; all three went to Old Oak Common depot initially. In one of those quirks which crop up occasionally, the trio all moved on from 81A to Newton Abbot on the same day – 30th March 1964 – at least on paper, and then from there to Laira on 10th July 1965. D1030's transfer to Bristol in September 1966 broke up the little group and then D1031's move to Landore in November 1968 really fragmented the trio. D1030 was the first of the class to be painted blue, known as Chromatic Blue, it was slightly different from the Rail blue which would become the standard; six other Westerns were also painted in the Chromatic scheme before the March 1967 'standard' was implemented. Note that all of these Crewe-built machines had headboard clips fitted. This particular view at Reading is no longer possible because of the rebuilding works which have taken place in recent years.

D1031 WESTERN RIFLEMAN is seen entering Liskeard with 4A07, the 14.45 Penzance to Paddington vans and parcels train on Sunday 1st September 1974. Liskeard is the junction for the delightful branch to Looe which is still very busy during the summer months.

D1032 WESTERN MARKSMAN passes Victoria Park, Bedminster, on its way to Temple Meads with 1A31 to Paddington on 7th June 1969; the locomotive had just been released from Swindon Works after overhaul and a repaint into the standard blue livery. This view is no longer possible due to the bush growth etc. D1032 went out of service early – the first of the Crewe batch to be withdrawn – she was condemned during May 1973 but was cut up at its spiritual home, Swindon.

D1033 WESTERN TROOPER under the wires at Birmingham New Street on 24th April 1976. Having arrived in the second city with the 14.05 ex Paddington, the Western is running round its train ready for the return journey back to London. This tiny corner of New Street was one of the few areas of the original station to survive the massive rebuilding of the Sixties'.

D1034 WESTERN DRAGOON about to enter Taunton with 1B73, the 14.30 Paddington to Paignton express on 3rd July 1975; I see from my records that I took this train as far as Newton Abbot. D1034 was the last of the Crewe batch and along with D1030 to D1033 should have actually been built at Swindon but for various reasons – cost, time, etc. – Swindon could not accommodate them whereas Crewe had some spare capacity as they were finishing off D1073 prior to beginning to erect the first lot of their Brush Type 4s (47s) D1550 onwards. However, D1034 entered traffic on 25th April 1964, nearly four months after D1033 was released from Crewe on 3rd January 1964.

D1035 WESTERN YEOMAN departs from Gloucester over Tramway Crossing, which, on this bright but very cold winters day – 3rd February 1969 – is under a light carpet of a snow. The train is 1B51, the morning Paddington to Cheltenham service, and maroon livery with the small yellow warning panel is the order of the day. The railway yards to the right of the picture are long gone but the Cathedral is still in place, also in the background can be seen the long footbridge which connected Eastgate and Central stations; Eastgate was still open at this time and was combined with Central. However, closure of the former Midland station took place in December 1975 and the GWR essentially won the battle of Gloucester which had been going on for a century. If any of the class was equipped with an appropriate name for future traffic purposes, it was this example surely!

D1036 WESTERN EMPOROR at Cardiff (General) on Tuesday 9th September 1975. The train is 1A51, the 15.30 Cardiff to Paddington via Gloucester service; note the incorrect head code from a previous working! During this period – with twenty-seven of the class already condemned – several of the surviving members were displaying some very washed-out paintwork. Of course, by this time Swindon was no longer carrying out any overhauls, repairs and accompanying repaints; these were instead being taken care of by Laira depot in Plymouth. D1036 was the recipient of one of these '83D' or should that be 84A? paint jobs and very nice it looked too. My records also tell me that I travelled behind D1036 all the way from Cardiff to Paddington.

D1037 WESTERN EMPRESS: with no excuse required for using another view at Fairwood Junction Westbury, this image reveals D1037 on 6th July 1974 on another stone working, albeit with a train of empty wagons headed to Westbury yards. D1037 looks very smart but it was not long after a Laira paint job, however there is already evidence of staining on the locomotives' body side. This Western, along with D1004 and D1036, managed to retain the green livery throughout the 1960s when all the others in the class were changed to maroon and blue.

D1038 WESTERN SOVEREIGN, stabled at Horton Road depot on Sunday 30th April 1972. This Western was another early casualty, being taken out of service in August 1973, withdrawn in October, and cut up at Swindon during November 1974.

(*above*) D1039 WESTERN KING at Bristol (Temple Meads) on 12th July 1969, awaiting the signal to take it onto the platform line to couple with – and head back home to Plymouth – 1V82, the 10.25 Manchester to Penzance Inter-Regional express. The locomotive is in the attractive maroon livery with the full yellow front end warning panels. At this period, the Peaks and Class 47s were not so common in the West Country because a lot of trains changed engines at Bristol. D1039 was the other member of the class used for the marine-type front screen wiper experiment; although there is no sign of that equipment by this date.

(*below*) D1040 WESTERN QUEEN at Horton Road Depot Gloucester on 2nd March 1970, in maroon livery with the small front end yellow warning panels. D1040 was a little over eleven months old when it was involved in a fatal crash at Knowle and Dorridge whilst hauling the BIRMINGHAM PULLMAN, from Snow Hill to Paddington on 15th August 1963. Sadly three people lost their lives as a result of this crash which occurred around 1:10pm whilst the train was travelling at high speed and was in collision with a freight train, which had been allowed out onto the main line in the path of the express. D1040 was eventually repaired and returned to service.

D1041 WESTERN PRINCE stands in the goods yard at Truro on the 3rd July 1975. Because of its well-worn paint work, D1041 had quite a following of Western fans during its latter days working for BR but internally it was in good condition and performed very well. Happily PRINCE is also preserved and can be seen on the East Lancashire Railway at Bury, where it works passenger services on the ELR from time to time.

43

D1042 WESTERN PRINCESS is seen powering along the sea wall at Teignmouth on a very dull Saturday 26th July 1969. The locomotive is in the maroon livery with small front-end warning panels. It was not until September that D1042 got it's all over blue livery being one of the last of the class to get that treatment again. It was quite an early withdrawal from service being condemned in July 1973 along with D1039.

D1043 WESTERN DUKE stands at Liskeard in charge of 1Z38, an excursion from Gloucester to Penzance. Being a Sunday this special gave me the chance of a day in the Duchy chasing the Westerns. I remember getting several of them in between stations and ending up in Penzance to get D1043 on its return.

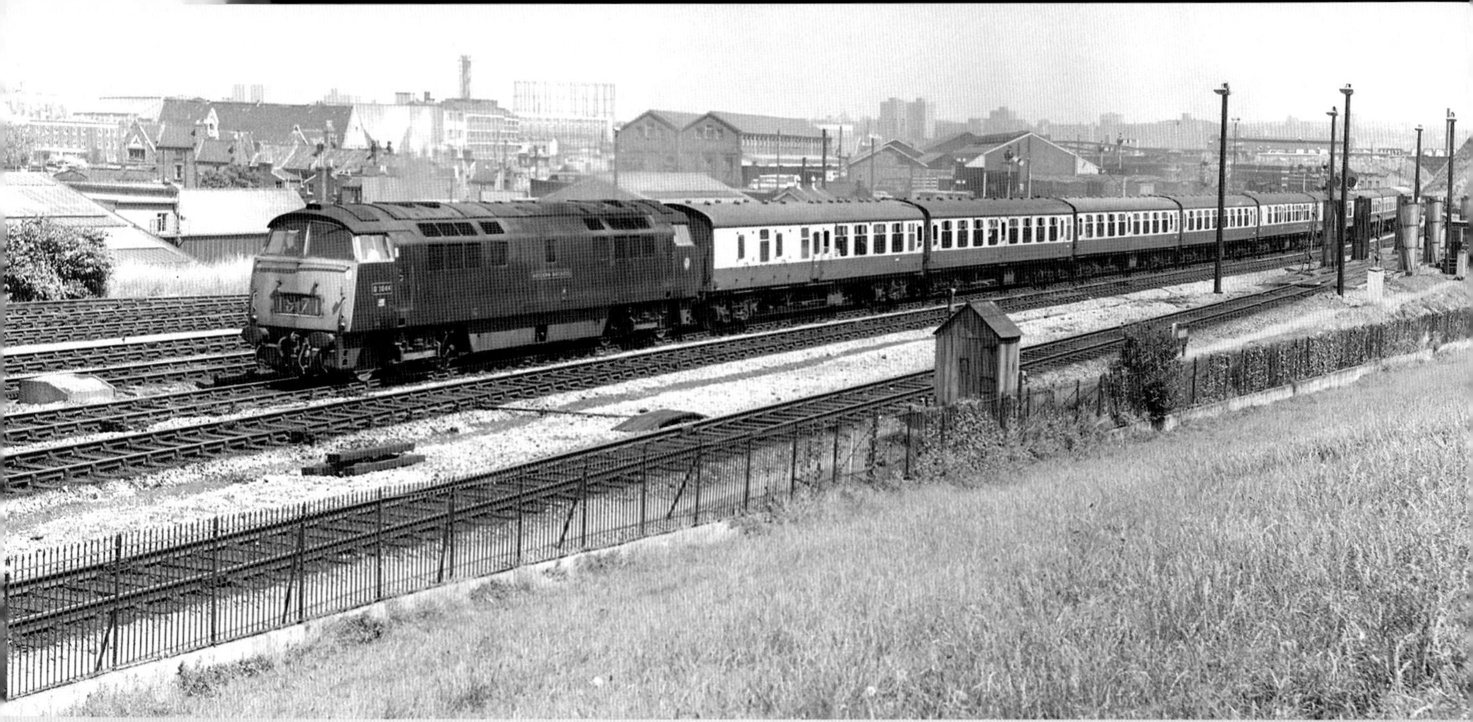

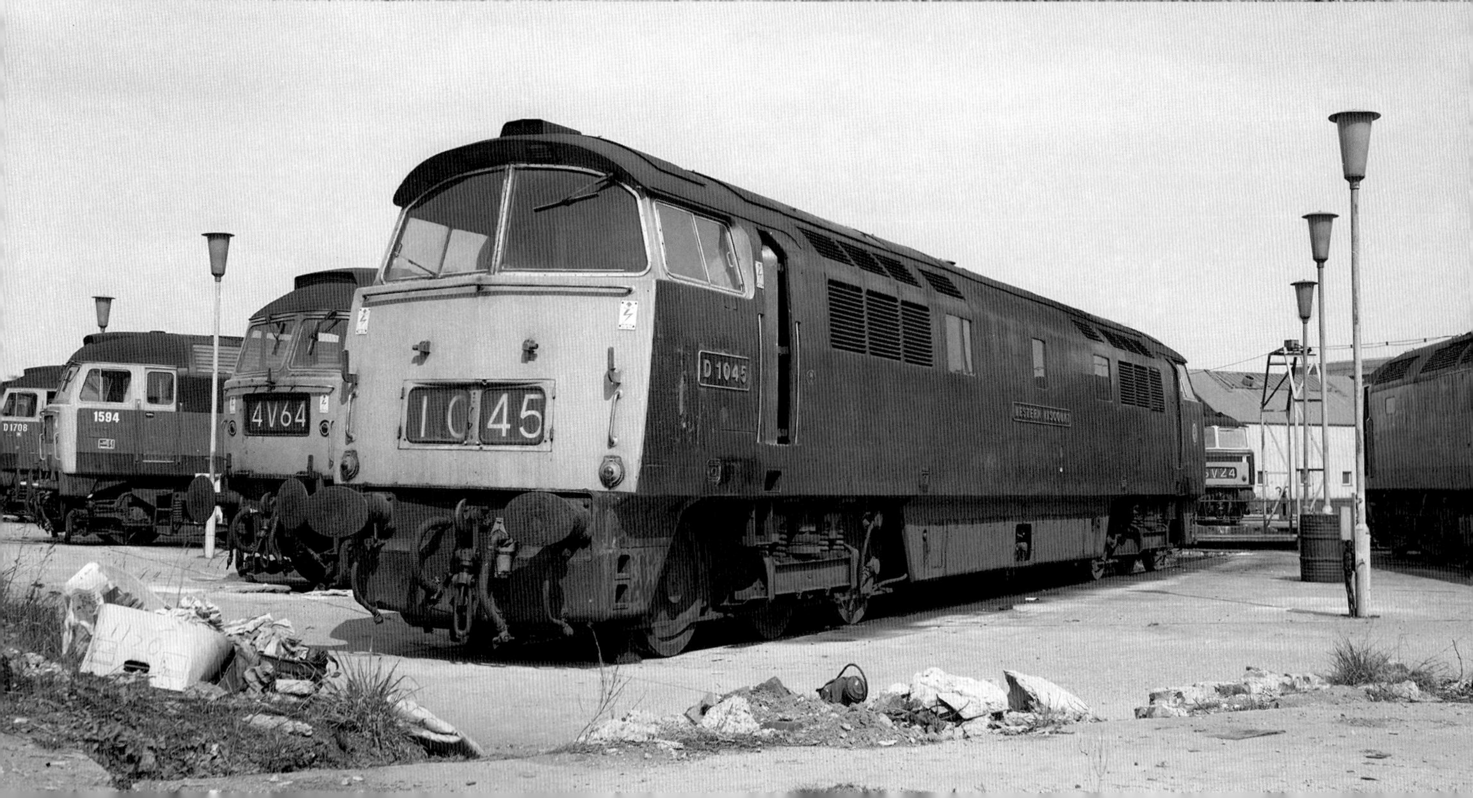
D1708
1594
4V64
D 1045

(*opposite*) **D1044 WESTERN DUCHESS** passing Victoria Park, Bedminster on the way out of Bristol with 1V71 Inter-Regional express to the West Country on Saturday 12th July 1969. D1044 is in the maroon livery with full yellow ends.

(*opposite, bottom*) **D1045 WESTERN VISCOUNT** takes a rest in between duties at Old Oak Common depot on 19th April 1969. Once again maroon livery and full yellow ends are the order of the day. Old Oak was a splendid location to photograph locomotives in close-up and if one asked permission of the Depot Foreman, one was not often refused. A Hymek and Brush Class 47 are stabled nearby.

D1046 WESTERN MARQUIS arrives at Exeter (St Davids) platform 2 during the afternoon of 15th July 1972 on what proved to be another sun filled day In Devon! The Western is in charge of 1V86, the 09.55 service from Bradford (Forster Square) to Paignton. No doubt the holidaymakers on board, heading to Torquay and Paignton, will be hoping that the weather holds for their annual holidays. Note the platform awning above the train which is fairly clean for much of its length but over the area where locomotives come to rest at the station stop, the paintwork is non-existent and is soot encrusted; much like the front of D1046.

47

D1047 WESTERN LORD rounds the curve which will take it out onto the sea wall at Teignmouth on 15th July 1972. D1047 is in charge of service 1A65, the 08.40 working from Penzance to Paddington.

D1048 WESTERN LADY arrives at journeys end in Paignton on 11th July 1976, the last full year of Western workings. The train is the 09.00 ex-Bristol and again will have a compliment of happy holidaymakers on board. Note that D1048 has its number displayed in the head codes panel box. One of the stand-by pair for the final tour – THE WESTERN TRIBUTE – of 26th February 1977, D1048 was one of the last of the class to remain in the service. She too is preserved.

D1049 WESTERN MONARCH approaches Didcot at speed with 1A43, the 08.53 Swansea to Paddington train on 27th October 1973. Note that D1049 has lost its headboard clips at this end! The cooling towers of Didcot 'A' power station can be seen in the background although some of these have recently been demolished to change the once familiar skyline.

D1050 WESTERN RULER is nearly at the end of its journey as it approaches West Ealing on 22nd February 1975 in charge of 1A35 the early morning 06.55 Plymouth to Paddington service. This Western started life at Canton depot on 19th January 1963 but transferred to Newton Abbot on 14th September 1964 as more of the new Brush type 4s were drafted into South Wales. It moved to Plymouth on 10th July 1965. West Ealing was another good location for pictures with plenty of trains to photograph, both passenger and freight.

D1051 WESTERN AMBASSADOR at St Austell on 24th August 1975. The train is 1B15, the 10.30 Paddington to Penzance express. At one time this station was the terminus for the motor rail services which ran from Kensington in West London and which were designed to attract motorists from the seasonally congested, not to mention poor, 'A' roads (the West Country was not served by any motorways at that time, and the Duchy still hasn't got a motorway of its own) and therefore save a long drive to Cornwall.

D1052 WESTERN VICEROY arrives at Reading from London with 1B83 the 15.30 service from Paddington to Penzance on 16th April 1974. Much was written about the choice of names for this class at the time of their entry into traffic, during their service for BR and indeed since their demise. The popularity of the class amongst railway enthusiasts is undiminished even when the names issue is raised. The writers of the names subject fall into two camps – the negatives, and the positives. It would not be an untruth to say that the former was the largest group, and probably still is. A story goes around that the author of the names wrote all seventy-four down on a single piece of foolscap paper one Friday afternoon whilst waiting for the end of his working week. Not quite $E=Mc^2$ material but bordering on the limits of believability. Genius or folly – you decide!?

D1053 WESTERN PATRIARCH runs a Down express around one of the curves at Teignmouth on 22nd June 1974. The external condition of many of the class was by this time looking decidedly scruffy, and it was not going to get any better. D1053 was part of a batch destined for Canton depot direct from Crewe in February 1963 but it spent its first month at Old Oak Common before joining D1049 to D1056 at Cardiff. Further members of the class migrated to Canton during that four month period from February to May 1963, D1035, D1037 to D1048, and D1057 to D1059 boosting the presence of the class in the Welsh capital. D1060 to D1064 joined them in late May and June. Of course, others joined them before and afterwards but during the first six months of 1963 approximately 80% of the class worked from Cardiff.

D1054 WESTERN GOVERNOR approaches Teignmouth past a group of holidaymakers out for a morning stroll before lunch on Saturday 22nd June 1974. The sea is in close proximity to the railway here and waves often come up over the trains during high tides and storms. In the background can be seen Parsons tunnel with the outcrop of rock, which made that bore necessary, protruding out into the ocean. D1054 is working 1B05, the 08.30 Paddington to Penzance service.

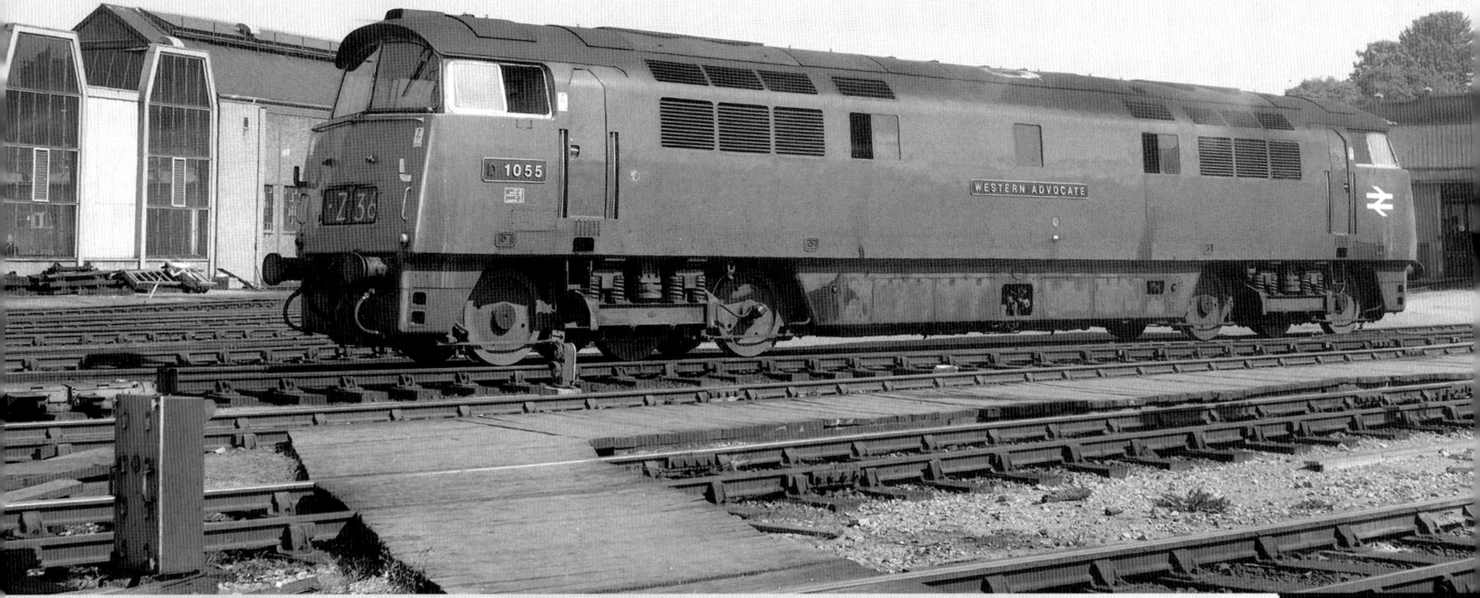
1055
WESTERN ADVOCATE

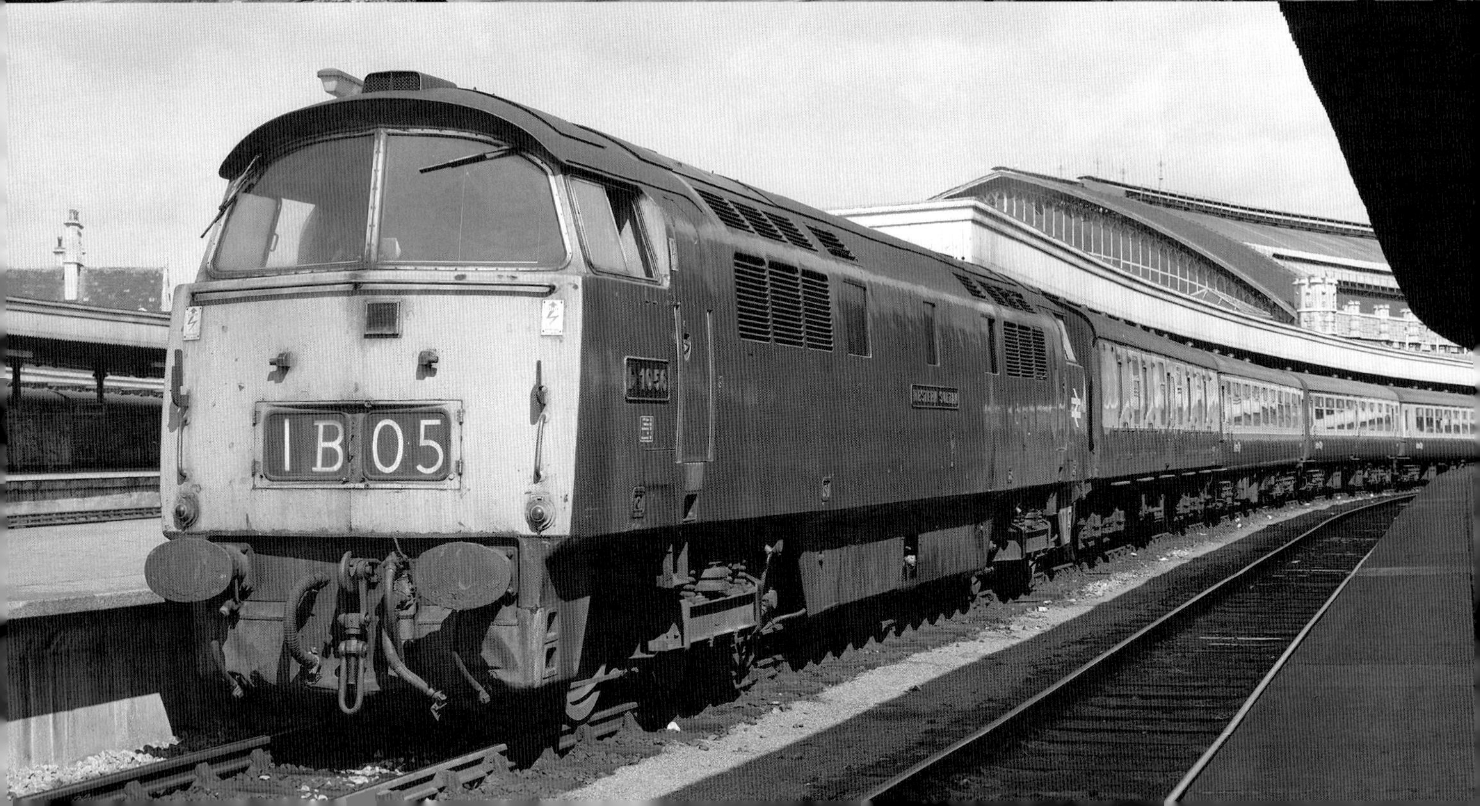
1B05

(*above*) **D1055 WESTERN ADVOCATE** at Bath Road depot on 7th June 1969; the Landore based C-C is looking fairly smart. Temple Meads station was a good location for observing and photographing all the comings and goings, on and off the depot. D1055 met its end in a fatal crash at Worcester Tunnel Junction when it collided with the rear of a parcels train on 3rd January 1976. The wrecked locomotive was immediately condemned and then stored at Worcester for some time afterwards before being taken to Swindon where it was eventually cut up during the following June.

(*below*) **D1056 WESTERN SULTAN** at Bristol (Temple Meads) whilst working the 08.35 Paddington to Plymouth via Bristol service on 17th August 1975. D1056 was also fitted with the cab ventilation system as part of the experiment, as can be seen by the square box on the front face.

D1057 WESTERN CHIEFTAIN departs from its Dawlish stop where it was booked from 10.56 until 10.58 with 1A59, the 9.50 Plymouth to Paddington express on 2nd August 1975. A group of Western fans, enjoying D1057 getting under way, are seen at the front coach window. Looking at the number of bodies revealed reminds me about how many people you can get inside a Mini – one of the proper ones?!

D1058 WESTERN NOBLEMEN arrives at journeys end, Penzance – some 326 miles or thereabouts covered – with 1B45, the 11.30 ex Paddington service on 28th March 1975. That particular day started very sunny but by lunchtime, rain, and even snow, had set in with bursts of sunlight from time to time. D1058 had run through some snow en route and it can be seen caked onto the front of the locomotive. The sea appears very calm but for how long? In the background the Long Rock stabling point and carriage cleaning facility can be seen. The locomotive stabling point, with its 1914-built engine shed, went out of use at virtually the same time as the Westerns went out of service.

(*opposite, top*) D1059 WESTERN EMPIRE powers through Dawlish Warren in charge of 1B65, the 13.30 Paddington to Penzance service on 28th August 1973. Living up to its seasonal trends, the car park is very full indicating that good trade is being done at the amusement arcade and nearby café, not to mention the very nice beach with its soft sand! Dawlish Warren is a quiet spot even today but sadly there are no Westerns passing at regular intervals.

(*opposite, bottom*) D1060 WESTERN DOMINION stands on Horton Road depot Gloucester in June 1970. Taken out of service during November 1973, along with D1024, D1060 was cut up at Swindon Works in the following July. Class leader D1000 was cut up in that same month, the pair being amongst the earliest victims of the 'Western' cull.

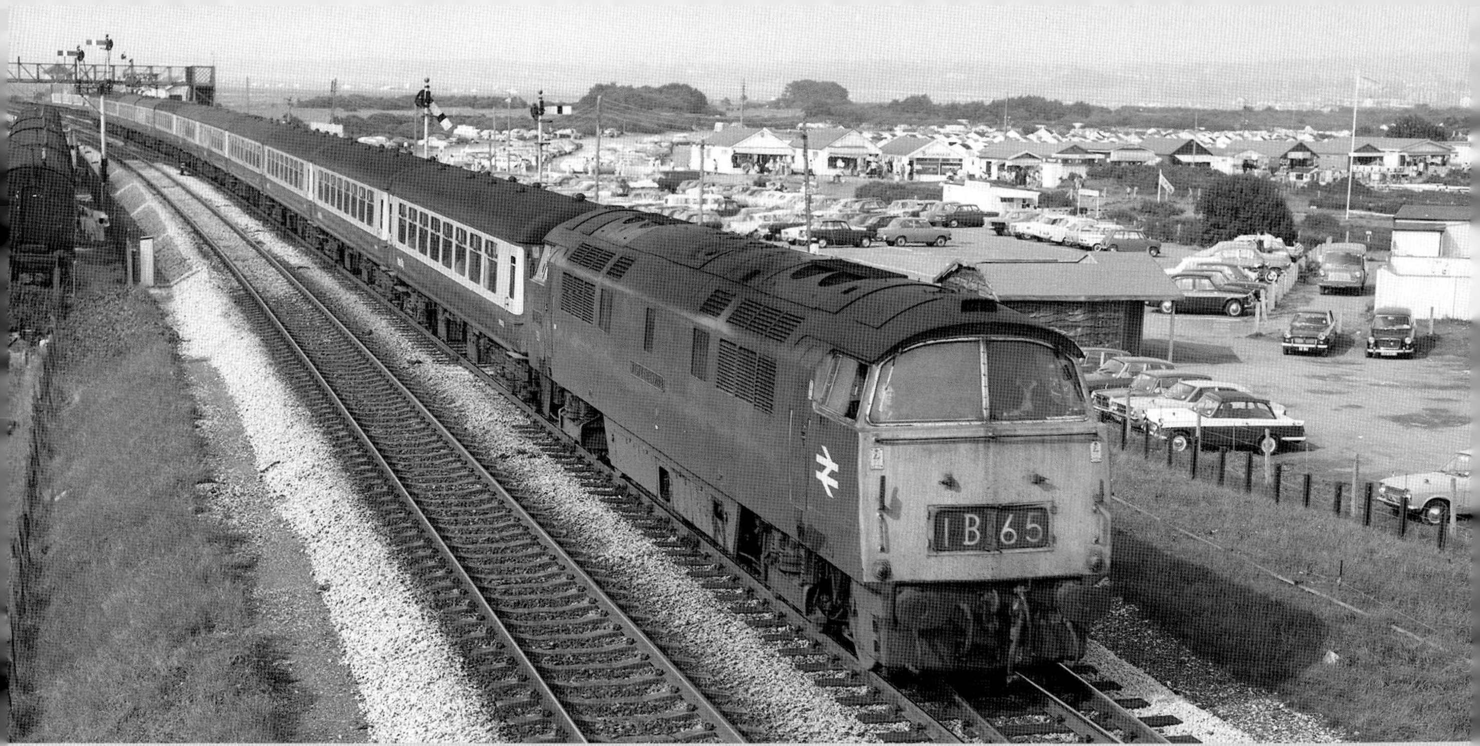
1B 65

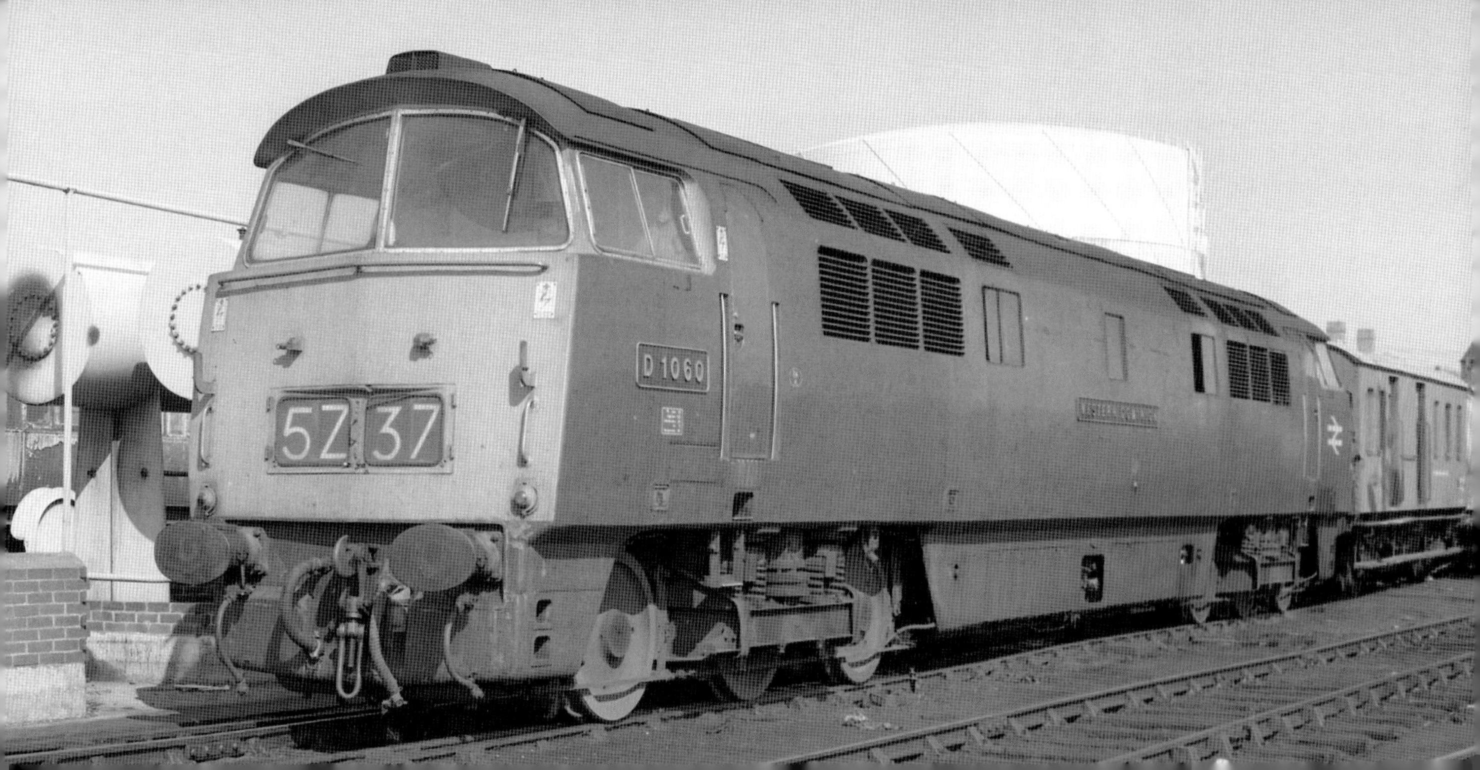
D 1060
5Z 37

D1061 WESTERN ENVOY is threading its way through the western suburbs of Plymouth and has just passed St. Budeaux station and is about to cross the Royal Albert bridge over the River Tamar into Cornwall. The train is 1V71, the 07.00 Bradford (Forster Square) to Penzance service on Saturday 15th June 1974. The Western would have taken over this train at Bristol (Temple Meads), the originating motive power, a Brush 47 or perhaps even a Class 46 'Peak' having been removed and taken to Bath Road depot for servicing. Note the apparent 'wrong-line working' here which preceded the singling of the route from St Budeaux (Ferry Road) station to the bridge approach on the Devon side; with the already single line section across the bridge to Saltash, there is now about a mile of single line.

D1062 WESTERN COURIER about to pass Dawlish Warren on the 12.20 Penzance to Paddington service 1A45 on 25th July 1974. In the background can be seen Langstone Rock which also made a good location from which to take photographs. D1062 was purchased by the Western Locomotive Association and it made its first run in preservation on 31st July 1977 whilst at the Paignton and Dartmouth Railway, and taking part in the working of a RPPR special organised by 'Western' fan and railway Author John Vaughn. The special had originated at Paddington and had travelled to Paignton via Bristol with 37s Nos.37269 and 37297 in charge. D1062 was finished in the maroon livery with small half yellow warning panels, as it would have carried in early BR days. The 'Western' took over for the Paignton-Dartmouth section, and return, with the 37s running the tour back to London. D1062 is now based at Severn Valley Railway where it can be seen at work from time to time.

D1063 WESTERN MONITOR at Plymouth on 1st February 1975 after arrival on 1Z15 – a relief from Paddington – is now running back to Laira depot for servicing. These relief trains were very popular with 'Western' fans as quite often they did produce a Western, and normally they called at the same stations as the main train.

D1064 WESTERN REGENT seen from the top of Langstone rock as mentioned in a previous caption. The train is 1B25, the 09.30 Paddington to Penzance and the date is 24th May 1975. At this time on a Saturday morning the lucky photographer could get three Western-hauled trains out of Paddington for the West Country: the 09.30 to Penzance, the 09.50 to Newquay and then the 10.30 to Paignton! Wait around for another hour, and, if your luck was in, the 11.30 from Paddington to Penzance would appear. Western heaven!? The bridge which can be seen in the top right of this illustration was the location used to record the image of D1062 WESTERN COURIER on the Up London train.

D1065 WESTERN CONSORT at the stabling point in Westbury on 3rd April 1976; the staff at Westbury were very good and moved locomotives around for me to get this 'set up' picture; the other Westerns being used in the production were D1001 WESTERN PATHFINDER and D1013 WESTERN RANGER. As mentioned before, Westbury was something of a 'hot spot' for Western activity in the latter years of their lives. D1013 lasted to the end during the following February and entered preservation whereas the other two were condemned before 1976 was out and entered Swindon never to come out except in little pieces.

D1066 WESTERN PREFECT runs past Cowley Bridge junction Exeter, with 1B55, the 12.30 Paddington to Paignton on 29th June 1974. The line to the left – singled now – went off to Meldon Quarry and Oakhampton; the former Southern Railway route through to Plymouth, north Devon, and Cornwall. Had it been intact it would have been an alternative to the GWR main line, and one that would have been more than useful when the seawall at Dawlish was breached in 2014. However, practicalities do not come into the equation when money and railways are mentioned nowadays. The very attractive half-timbered Cowley Bridge Inn is seen above the locomotive.

D1067 WESTERN DRUID brings us back to the sea wall near Teignmouth, this time we are a little nearer to the resort town. The Western has charge of 1B18, the 09.45 Cardiff to Paignton express on 16th June 1973. Though the locomotive was appropriately named to haul a train originating in Wales, I wonder if any of the passengers noticed the 'connection?' The sea mist covering the banks nearer Parsons Tunnel was a regular phenomenon which often occurred on hot, still mornings before the summer sun had got to work.

D1068 WESTERN RELIANCE at Fishguard harbour on 17th July 1976. D1068 had arrived with the Saturdays only (SO) 08.25 ex-Paddington and had now run round its train for the 14.30 departure to Paddington via Swansea. On the outward run the train travelled via the Swansea District lines, and was non-stop from Cardiff to Fishguard where a connection was made with the Irish ferry to Rosslare. On its return, this train went into Swansea where a reversal was made and the working became a Swansea to Paddington service, although not often with a Western in charge. More than often, a Brush class 47 would be used with D1068 then having to go to Landore depot. This train was always keenly watched by the Western haulage men as this was the only – once a week – chance to get to Fishguard with a Western. The train did not produce a Western very often and I only went there a handful of times in the season. I will always remember the fare from Cardiff to Fishguard which was the princely sum of £5.00 and 1p – return. Happy days indeed!

D1069 WESTERN VANGUARD powers through Sonning with 1V41, the 13.25 Birmingham (New Street) to London (Paddington) express on 5th July 1975. This would be the final summer of working for D1069, the Crewe-built example being withdrawn during the following October. It was cut up in the same month that the remaining members of the Western class were withdrawn from service on BR.

D1070 WESTERN GUANTLET gives us a last look in this album of Fairwood Junction signal box, and the elm trees, as the big diesel takes the line into Westbury for a scheduled stop whilst in charge of 1A69, the 10.30 from Plymouth to Paddington service on Saturday 30th March 1974.

D1071 WESTERN RENOWN has just been released from its train at Paddington and will follow the empty carriage working down to Old Oak Common for servicing in readiness for its next duty. Again the experimental ventilation box is seen to good effect. A tripod and a long time exposure were used to capture this view, on the night of Saturday 25th October 1975.

D1072 WESTERN GLORY is seen heading for Paddington and passing Southall with 12.00 Paignton to Paddington express on 7th August 1976. The head code box now carries the locomotive number which was a grand idea. In the background a diesel multiple unit stopping service from Reading is making slow progress on its way into Paddington which is just a few more stops away.

D1073 WESTERN BULWARK is coming off Bath Road depot Bristol in order to take over 1V60 to the West Country on 12th July 1969. In the background can be seen an office block being constructed to the period design! Over the ensuing years the vista here has changed somewhat. The office block is now disused, and Bath Road depot, like our subject locomotive, is pure history.